I SELF Body Health/Fitness
Power

Power, Teresa Anne
ABCs of Yoga for Kids Around
the World
12/12/17

the ABCs of YOGA for KiDS AROUND the WORLD

written by Teresa Anne Power

illustrated by Kathleen Rietz

STAFFORD HOUSE BOOKS, INC.

The ABCs of Yoga for Kids Around the World
Written by Teresa Anne Power
Illustrated by Kathleen Rietz
Copyright © 2017

ISBN: 978-0-9822587-8-1

Publisher's Cataloging-In-Publication Data
(Prepared by The Donohue Group, Inc.)

Names: Power, Teresa Anne. | Rietz, Kathleen, illustrator.
Title: The ABCs of yoga for kids around the world / written by Teresa Anne Power ; illustrated by Kathleen Rietz.
Description: Pacific Palisades, CA : Stafford House Books, Inc., [2017] | Interest age level: 003-008. | Summary: "The ABCs of Yoga for Kids around the World is a fun-filled tour of 32 countries, introducing kid-friendly, easy-to-learn yoga poses along the way. A follow-up to the bestselling The ABCs of Yoga for Kids and written in honor of International Kids Yoga Day, this book features beautiful illustrations, charming rhymes, and fun facts about this wonderful world in which we live."--Provided by publisher.
Identifiers: ISBN 978-0-9822587-8-1
Subjects: LCSH: Hatha yoga for children. | Exercise for children. | Yoga--Juvenile literature. | Exercise--Juvenile literature. | Geography--Miscellanea--Juvenile literature. | Alphabet books. | CYAC: Yoga. | Exercise. | Geography--Miscellanea. | LCGFT: Stories in rhyme.
Classification: LCC RJ133.7 .P692 2017 | DDC 613.7/046083--dc23

For more information contact:
Stafford House, P.O. Box 291, Pacific Palisades, CA 90272
www.staffordhousebooks.com

Book Design by Dotti Albertine
Map illustrations by iStock, Getty Images

Printed in China on acid-free paper

Also by Teresa Anne Power:

The ABCs of Yoga for Kids
(also available in Spanish, French, Italian and Danish)

The ABCs of Yoga for Kids Coloring Book

The ABCs of Yoga for Kids: A Guide for Parents and Teachers

The ABCs of Yoga for Kids Learning Cards

The ABCs of Yoga for Kids Poster

INTRODUCTION

In 2016, I founded the international *Kids' Yoga Day* as a way to raise global awareness of the importance of our youth's health and fitness through yoga. **Over 25,000 children in 46 states and 21 countries participated in its inaugural year by practicing 5 minutes of yoga on the same day and at the same time.**

The result was magic. At 11:00 AM local time at schools, yoga studios, and child care organizations throughout the world, official "ambassadors," plus countless others who followed along at home, led students through a specially designed 5-minute yoga routine based on my first book, *The ABCs of Yoga for Kids*. After they completed the routine, the children received a special certificate of completion and a copy of the 5-minute routine to practice all year round.

The tremendous success of *Kids' Yoga Day* inspired me to write this book to further call attention to this worthy cause. If our next generation can learn to calm themselves, while at the same time building strength and fortitude, our world will be a better place. *The ABCs of Yoga for Kids Around the World* celebrates both our diversity and oneness at the same time.

There are 195 countries in the world plus about 60 dependent areas. This book is an alphabetical listing of many of these regions; for bonus material regarding other countries and territories go to **www.abcyogaforkids.com**. There is no country starting with the letter X; I took the liberty of including Xion, a famous ancient capital of China, in order to complete the alphabet format. Have fun learning about different areas of the world and practicing some simple yoga poses at the same time!

Yours in health,
Teresa Anne Power

Aa
is for Australia

Gi'day from the land down under and home of the koala bear.

KOALA

Standing up with my hands and feet on the ground,
I look forward, not making a sound.
Next, I begin to walk using opposite hands and feet.
Stretching my body is such a treat!
I bring my left leg forward and then my right arm.
I am a koala, full of charm.

Bb
is for Brazil

Ola from this Portuguese speaking country that is home to many kinds of beautiful birds, the largest of which is the rhea.

RHEA

To become a beautiful rhea bird,
I must be calm and centered.
Standing tall, I bend one leg and bring my foot inside my thigh,
As I give balancing on one leg a try.
Next I tilt forward with my hands in prayer position behind my back,
Keeping my spine straight, not with a hunched back.
A wondrous, flightless bird am I,
Balancing with my neck forward and my chin held high.

Cc
is for Canada

Bonjour from Canada, where French and English are the official languages, and which is home to the Canadian lynx, a medium-sized cat.

CAT

My hands and knees on the floor,
I become a cat.
Stretching one leg to form a tail,
I say "Meow," just like that!

Cc
is for China

Ni Hao from China, home of the endangered Yangtze alligator
and where paper, kites and soccer were invented.

ALLIGATOR
Resting on my belly,
A hungry alligator am I.
Open and shut go my palms
As I snap at everything nearby.

Dd
is for Denmark

Hej from this Scandinavian country known for its whirling windmills.

WINDMILL

Standing with legs slightly bent and my feet wide apart,
I bring one hand down to the ground in line with my heart.
Sending my other arm up toward the sky,
I extend it long and keep reaching up high.
Switching arms on the count of three,
I am a windmill, twirling and carefree.

Ee
is for Egypt

Marhaba from this Mediterranean country where Egyptian Arabic is spoken and which is home to the mysterious Sphynx of Giza.

SPHYNX

The Egyptian Sphynx is part lion and part man.
Made of stone, I lie still on my belly in the sand.
With legs straight and forearms pressed firmly into the ground,
I look forward, frozen in time, without making a sound.

Ff
is for France

Bonjour from France, where you can walk across the world's tallest suspension bridge, climbing higher than the Eiffel Tower.

BRIDGE

Lying on my back and bending my knees,
I lift my hips high, forming a bridge, and then I just breathe.
With my arms underneath me straight along the floor,
I press into my shoulders as I raise my body a little bit more.

Gg
is for Greece

Yassas from Greece, where dolphins have been a part of Greek civilization for over 3,000 years. Their playful images appear on many ancient wall paintings, pottery, coins, and jewelry.

DOLPHIN

I am a dolphin who loves to swim in the sea.
I sit on my heels with my arms stretched in front of me.
Straightening my legs, I keep my forearms on the floor,
Looking at my feet so my neck doesn't get sore.

Gg
is for Guam

Hafa Adai from Guam, an island country in the Pacific Ocean where Chamorro is spoken and the beautiful bougainvillea is the state flower.

FLOWER

I am a beautiful flower growing in the sun.
Just as my yoga teacher said it would be,
Yoga is so much fun!
Sitting with the soles of my feet touching,
Careful that my back is not hunching,
I lift my legs and bring my arms beneath my knees.
Balancing on my seat, I count to three.

Hh
is for Hungary

Szia from Budapest, the capital of Hungary, where you might meet a Vizsla, a type of Hungarian hunting dog.

DOG

I am a dog stretching after a nap.
On my hands and knees, I begin to yap.
Straightening my legs and lifting my hips,
I spread each and every one of my fingertips.
Looking down, I can see my toes,
As I focus on breathing in and out through my nose.

Ii
is for India

Namaste from India, where yoga began over 5,000 years ago. The peacock is the national bird of India and is a symbol of grace, joy, beauty, and love.

PEACOCK

I am a colorful peacock sitting proud and tall.
My back is so straight it's like I'm sitting against a wall.
I spread my legs apart as far as they can comfortably go,
Feeling the stretch all the way from my head to my toes.

Ii
is for Italy

Buon giorno from Italy, where you can hop with the Corsican hare, a rare animal found in the southern and central parts of the country.

HARE

I am a hare with long ears.
Jumping around, I have no fears.
Crouching low with my knees bent and parallel to the ground,
I keep my back flat as I gaze forward without a sound.
Bending my elbows, I place my forearms on the floor,
Getting ready to hop forward as I hold in my core.

Ii
is for Israel

Shalom from Israel, where you can eat delicious foods like falafel and hummus and maybe meet a Middle East tree frog.

FROG

Squatting with my feet apart wide,
I am a frog with a big underside.
Bringing my arms inside my knees,
I jump up and say, "R-r-r-r-i-b-b-i-t!" on the count of three.

Jj
is for Japan

Konnichiwa from Japan, home to the beautiful cherry blossom trees which bloom in the spring and draw crowds of admiring people to parks, gardens and riversides.

TREE

I am an old and solid tree.
My roots grow deep into the ground beneath me.
Bending one leg, I bring my foot to my thigh.
Balancing can be tricky, but I'll give it a try!
I focus my sight on a single spot.
Yoga improves my concentration a lot.

Kk
is for Kenya

Jambo from Kenya, where Swahili is spoken and the African lion proudly roams the grasslands.

LION

I kneel on my shins with my chest on my thighs.
Getting ready to spring forward, I look to the sky.
I give a mighty roar on the count of three.
The new king of the jungle—yes, a lion, that's me!

LI
is for Liberia

Hello from Liberia, where you can find African elephants
and the official language is English.

ELEPHANT

A mighty and powerful elephant am I!
While standing, I fold forward and then lumber by.
Interlacing my hands and gently swinging my trunk,
I begin to move slowly, each step making a thunk.

Mm
is for Malaysia

Hello from the tropical islands of Malaysia, just north of the equator. In the surrounding sparkling ocean waters, you might spot whale, hammerhead, or reef sharks.

SHARK

I am a stealthy shark cruising through the sea.
I lie on my belly with my legs straight behind me.
My fingers interlace as I lift my arms and chest.
My fin can be seen by all as I ride a wave's crest.

Mm
is for Mexico

Hola from Mexico and its sandy, white beaches,
where sea turtles come to nest every year.

TURTLE

From a seated position, I bend my knees and open my legs wide.
I become a shy turtle carrying a shell in which to hide.
With my feet flat on the floor, I bring my arms under my knees,
Looking down toward my belly, I count "One-two-three!"
Then slowly lifting my head out of my shell,
I look up and see that the world around me is swell.

Nn
is for Norway

God dag from Norway, where the playful Eurasian otter
is a common sight along the coast.

OTTER

I am a playful otter chasing fish in the water.
Lying on my belly with my arms out in front,
I place my legs on the floor and extend them from my trunk.
Slowly pushing up, with my hands against the floor,
I lift my head and chest just a little bit more.

Oo
is for Oman

Marhaba from this Middle Eastern country, where you can find two of the six worldwide species of flamingos.

FLAMINGO

Standing tall I bend one leg and hold on to my knee.
Like a flamingo I balance, just as stable as can be.
With my eyes focused straight ahead I have tremendous poise.
I hold my stance silently, never making a noise.
First I balance on one side,
Then switch and give the other a try.

Pp
is for Peru

Hola from Peru, where the tiny marmoset monkey can be found playing in the Peruvian Amazon rain forest.

MONKEY

Standing tall I gaze straight ahead,
My arms are raised sideways and widespread.
I bring my legs apart shoulder wide.
I am a monkey full of pride.
Rotating my right foot and slightly bending my knee,
I bend my elbows and wrists and slowly count to three.
My palms face upward towards the sky,
As I focus front and let my imagination fly.

Qq
is for Qatar

Marhaba from Qatar, where you can watch an exciting
camel race or meet a desert hedgehog.

HEDGEHOG

To become a spiny hedgehog I lie with my back on the floor.
Next I bend my knees to my chest as I hold in my core.
Interlacing my hands around my legs, I inhale through my nose,
Then I exhale as I relax in this fun yoga pose.
Giving myself a hug, I bring my forehead to my knees.
Breathing deeply, I count to eight and freeze.

Rr
is for Russia

Zdras-tvuy-te from Russia, the largest-sized country in the world and home to many freshwater and marine fish.

FISH

I am a fish swimming deep in the sea.
Resting on my back I imagine the water all around me.
With my arms under my body, I lift my chest to the ceiling.
This truly is a magnificent feeling!
With the top of my head resting on the ground,
I look back without making a sound.

Ss
is for Spain

Hola from Spain, where over 563 species of birds fly high above the Pyrenees Mountains.

BIRD

High on my tiptoes I am a bird preparing to fly.
Flapping my wings repeatedly, I give flying a try!

Tt
is for Thailand

Sawaddee ka from Thailand, where the monocled cobra slithers throughout this tropical country in Southeast Asia.

COBRA

Hiss, hiss... I am a snake,
Lying on my belly in the sun to bake.
Elbows bent and close by my side,
I lift my chest, full of cobra pride.

Uu
is for United Kingdom

Hello from the United Kingdom, home to
Buckingham Palace and the royal family.

QUEEN

I am a royal queen,
Revered in such high esteem.
I stand tall and erect,
Making sure my breathing is correct.
With my shoulders back and head facing straight,
I slowly count to eight.

Uu
is for United States

Hello from the United States, where the bald eagle symbolizes freedom, long life, and great strength.

EAGLE

Standing tall I raise my arms above my head,
I am an eagle with my wings outspread.
I slowly hook my right arm underneath my left at the elbow,
Trying to cross my fingers together as I squat down low.
Slowly I bring my right leg over the left one and around it,
Yoga helps me become more flexible, bit by bit.
Gazing forward, I count to eight.
Eagle pose makes me feel so great!
Switching sides, I take it all in stride.

Vv
is for Vietnam

Chào from this eastern country in Southeast Asia, where the black-headed ibis can be found flying through marshy wetlands and on the coast.

IBIS

Standing quiet and still,
I am a beautiful ibis with a long down-curved bill.
Looking forward, I lift my right leg parallel to the floor.
Next I bring my arms behind me and count to four.
Balancing on my left leg,
I take a deep breath in through my nose,
Feeling the stretch from my head to my toes.

Ww
is for Western Sahara

Hola from this Spanish speaking territory in one of the world's largest hot deserts, covering most of North Africa. The desert monitor is a species of lizards found in Western Sahara.

LIZARD

Lying on my tummy I bend my elbows and look straight ahead.
I keep my back flat, with my fingers widespread.
Lifting my legs off the ground,
I bend one leg at the knee without making a sound.
Predators abound and keep me alert.
I am a monitor lizard living in the desert.

Xx
is for Xi'an

Ni Hao from Xi'an, one of the famous ancient capitals
of China and home to the Terracotta Warriors.

WARRIOR

I am a Terracotta Warrior,
Proud and strong.
I stand with feet wide apart,
And arms extended long.
Pointing my front toes straight ahead,
I bend my front knee.
Warrior Pose is a powerful posture,
As everyone can see!

Yy
is for Yemen

Marhaban from this Arab republic, which includes over 200 islands and 117 different species of colorful butterflies.

BUTTERFLY

With the soles of my feet touching I gaze straight ahead.
My hands rest on my shoulders as my butterfly wings spread.

Zz
is for Zimbabwe

Mhoro from Zimbabwe, where Victoria Falls is a majestic waterfall on the Zambezi River.

WATERFALL

Raising my arms up, I stand tall.
My body forms the shape of a flowing waterfall.
As I reach my fingertips to the sky,
I look toward my hands, held up high.
Extending back as far as I can comfortably go,
I let my mind and body begin to gently flow.

www.staffordhousebooks.com